This book belongs to:

____

19595559R00066

Made in the USA
Middletown, DE
06 December 2018